Stigma of Mental Health And Issues in the Anxious Generation: Discussing how Societal attitudes toward mental health affect anxiety and the willingness to seek help

By

Dr. Emily k Pitts

Disclaimer

Only informative material about mental health stigma and anxiety-related problems in the younger generation is available on this platform. It represents broad observations and conversations about how attitudes in society toward mental health impact anxiety and the propensity to seek assistance. It is not the intention of this information to serve as professional guidance or a replacement for speaking with licensed mental health specialists. For any queries or worries you may have regarding mental health, you should always seek the advice of a certified therapist, counselor, or healthcare professional.

About the Author

Renowned clinical psychologist, author, and educator Dr. Emily K. Pitts is well-known for her knowledge of mental health. Dr. Pitts, who received his Ph.D. in clinical psychology from Stanford University, has spent more than 20 years working in clinical settings and conducting research on anxiety disorders and the impact of society on mental health. Her most recent work, "Stigma of Mental Health and Issues in the Anxious Generation," explores the complex connection between the prevalence of anxiety in today's youth and cultural views regarding mental health. In her book, Dr. Pitts delves into the ways that stigma and misunderstandings about mental health can seriously impede people's willingness to ask for assistance. She offers a thorough explanation of how societal pressures and cultural narratives contribute to the rising anxiety levels in the younger generation by drawing on her considerable research and clinical expertise. Dr. Pitts highlights the pressing need to change how people view mental health disorders and to create an atmosphere that is more accepting and supportive of those who are experiencing them.Dr. Pitts is a well-known author and speaker who has given talks at numerous international conferences and had multiple publications published in prestigious psychological journals. Her work has been crucial in pushing for legislative improvements, increasing mental wellness, and improving public awareness of mental health. As she works to de-stigmatize mental health and assist those in need, Dr. Pitts never stops inspiring and educating others.

Table of Contents

- The Role of Media in Shaping Perceptions
- Cultural Differences in Mental Health Stigma
- The Impact of Social Media and Online Communities

Chapter 4: The Intersection of Stigma and Anxiety

- How Stigma Exacerbates Anxiety
- Case Studies: Personal Stories of Struggle and Resilience
- The Psychological Impact of Being Stigmatized

Chapter 5: Encouraging Help-Seeking Behavior

- Barriers to Seeking Help
- Strategies to Reduce Stigma and Promote Awareness
- Role of Education and Advocacy

Conclusion

Introduction to the Anxious Generation

Understanding the Modern Anxious Generation In recent years, the prevalence of anxiety disorders has skyrocketed, particularly among younger generations. Often nicknamed the "Anxious Generation," today's youth encounter a unique mix of difficulties that contribute to heightened feelings of anxiety. From the strains of social media to the uncertainties of economic instability and the global COVID-19 pandemic, several variables have collided to produce an environment ripe for mental health difficulties. Despite greater knowledge and discourse around mental health, a key obstacle remains: the stigma associated with mental health disorders.

Defining anxiety and mental health issues Anxiety disorders cover a range of ailments, including generalized anxiety disorder (GAD), panic disorder, social anxiety disorder, and specific phobias. These conditions are characterized by excessive dread, concern, and related behavioral problems. Mental health difficulties, more widely, can include depression, bipolar disorder, schizophrenia, and other psychiatric diseases that adversely influence an individual's emotional, psychological, and social well-being. The anxious generation grapples not just with these clinical disorders but also with subclinical anxiety—ppervasive concern and tension that, while not reaching the threshold of a diagnosable diagnosis, still severely influences daily life. The cumulative influence of these events is enormous, influencing everything from academic and professional performance to interpersonal relationships and physical health.

The Rise of Mental Health Awareness The past few decades have seen a remarkable growth in mental health awareness. Campaigns, educational programs, and popular personalities speaking out about their challenges have all led to a more open discourse about mental health. The development of social media has also played a key role in creating outlets for individuals to share their stories and find support. Despite these developments, stigma remains a strong impediment, often inhibiting individuals from obtaining the care they need.

Societal Changes and Their Impact on Mental Health Societal views towards mental health have progressed; however, stigma persists, entrenched in historical beliefs and cultural standards. While previous generations may have considered mental health concerns as indicators of personal weakness or moral failing, today's adolescents are more likely to see these issues from the perspective of medical and psychological science. However, this transformation is uneven throughout different civilizations, cultures, and even within groups, producing a complex landscape where stigma can flourish.

Historical Perspectives on Mental Health Stigma To properly comprehend the stigma surrounding mental health, it is vital to investigate its historical context. Mental health stigma is not a new phenomenon; it has existed for centuries and has been affected by cultural, religious, and scientific views many times. In ancient times, mental illness was typically linked to supernatural forces or moral failings, leading to therapies that ranged from exorcisms to isolation.

Evolution of Mental Health Treatment The evolution of mental health therapy reflects evolving attitudes regarding mental disease. The development of asylums in the 18th and 19th centuries signified a turn towards institutional care, but with often cruel conditions. The 20th century brought improvements in psychiatric therapy, including the discovery of psychotropic drugs and the deinstitutionalization movement, which tried to integrate individuals with mental health concerns back into the community. Despite these achievements, the legacy of historical cruelty and ignorance continues, contributing to persistent stigma. Modern mental health advocacy efforts attempt to overcome these historical narratives by fostering understanding, empathy, and evidence-based therapies.

Societal Attitudes and Their Impact Societal attitudes regarding mental health are impacted by several variables, including media representations, cultural standards, and generational disparities. The media plays a key role in either supporting or combating mental health stigma. Sensationalized portrayals of mental illness in movies, television, and news can reinforce negative preconceptions, while more nuanced and truthful depictions can foster understanding and empathy. Cultural variations can play a critical role in developing views towards mental health. In some cultures, mental health concerns are strongly stigmatized and considered a cause of shame for the individual and their family. This can lead to underreporting and a reluctance to seek help. In various cultures, there is a rising acknowledgment of mental health as a valid and vital element of general well-being. Generational differences in views are obvious, with younger generations generally demonstrating increased openness to discussing mental health issues. However, this openness may not always translate to reduced stigma or an increased desire to seek treatment. The fear of being judged or misunderstood by peers, family, and society at large can still operate as a substantial deterrent.

The role of social media and online communities Social media and online groups have a dual impact on mental health stigma. On one side, they provide forums for individuals to share their experiences, receive support, and obtain information. Online groups can offer a sense of belonging and lessen feelings of loneliness for those battling with mental health concerns. On the other side, social media can also heighten anxiety and contribute to the persistence of stigma. The temptation to offer a controlled, idealized version of oneself can lead to increased stress and feelings of inadequacy. Cyberbullying and online harassment are additional hazards that can have significant mental health implications.

The Intersection of Stigma and Anxiety The relationship between stigma and anxiety is bidirectional. Stigma can aggravate anxiety by establishing an environment of dread and humiliation. Individuals who internalize societal stigma may develop self-stigma when they perceive their mental health concerns as personal failures. This might lead to emotions of hopelessness, lower self-esteem, and increased worry. Conversely, anxiety itself can be stigmatized, with people being characterized as "overly sensitive" or "unable to cope." This can dissuade people from getting treatment since they may fear being judged or disregarded. The interaction of stigma and anxiety generates a vicious cycle where stigma raises anxiety, and anxiety, in turn, perpetuates stigma.

Case Studies: Personal Stories of Struggle and Resilience Personal tales and case studies provide vital insights into the real-life impact of stigma on individuals with anxiety. These accounts show the hardships experienced, the resilience demonstrated, and the significance of support and understanding. Case studies can serve as important tools for education and advocacy, helping to humanize mental health issues and reduce stigma.

Breaking the Cycle: Overcoming Internalized Stigma Overcoming internalized stigma is a vital step towards improved mental health outcomes. This involves confronting negative self-perceptions and replacing them with more realistic and compassionate perspectives. Therapy, support groups, and educational programs can all play a role in helping individuals overcome internalized stigma.

Encouraging Help-Seeking Behavior One of the most prominent repercussions of stigma is its discouraging effect on help-seeking behavior. Fear of being judged or stigmatized keeps many people from obtaining the mental health services they need. Reducing stigma and boosting help-seeking behavior requires a diverse strategy. #### Barriers to Seeking Help Several hurdles contribute to the unwillingness to seek care for mental health disorders. These include lack of awareness, fear of prejudice, and limited access to mental health services. Financial constraints, regional limitations, and cultural barriers can all play a role.

Strategies to Reduce Stigma and Promote Awareness Reducing stigma takes concerted efforts at several levels. Public education efforts can raise awareness and combat misunderstandings. Training programs for healthcare providers, educators, and employers can promote a more compassionate and knowledgeable approach to mental health. Encouraging open conversations about mental health.

Chapter.1

Comprehending the Contemporary Generation of Anxious People

A Comprehensive Examination of Anxiety and Related Mental Health Issues One of the most prevalent mental health issues in modern culture is anxiety disorder. Among these conditions are panic disorder, social anxiety disorder, generalized anxiety disorder (GAD), and various phobias. Anxiety by itself is a common and generally healthy emotion, but when it gets in the way of day-to-day activities and overall wellbeing, it becomes a problem. In the context of the current generation, anxiety disorders are notably more common. A combination of factors, including genetic predispositions and environmental stressors, are to blame for this. Rapid technological breakthroughs, cultural demands, and an unrelenting stream of information have created an environment that is conducive to anxiety. Millions of people worldwide suffer from generalized anxiety disorder, which is defined by persistent, excessive worry about a variety of life-related issues. The symptoms of generalized anxiety disorder (GAD) include irritation, weariness, restlessness, muscle tightness, difficulties concentrating, and disturbed sleep. On the other side, social anxiety disorder is characterized by a strong fear of social settings and other people's judgment. Avoidance habits may result from this, which can have a negative effect on one's social and professional life. Another common disorder is panic disorder, which is characterized by frequent, unplanned panic attacks. These episodes, which might involve palpitations, perspiration, shaking, shortness of breath, and a sense of impending doom, are abrupt bursts of extreme dread. It can be crippling to be afraid of having another panic attack, which frequently results in increased distress and loneliness. Other mental health issues that the younger generation is frequently dealing with include obsessive-compulsive disorder (OCD), bipolar disorder, and depression. Anxiety and depression can coexist, which makes diagnosis and therapy more difficult. Depression is characterized by enduring melancholy and interest loss. Mood swings associated with bipolar disorder include emotional highs (mania or hypomania) and lows (depression). Unwanted, repetitive thoughts (called obsessions) and actions (called compulsions) that the person feels compelled to carry out are characteristics of OCD.

The Amount of Awareness Regarding Mental Health

The last few decades have seen a notable rise in public understanding of mental health issues. This increased awareness has resulted from a number of factors, including public health initiatives, celebrity advocacy, the spread of knowledge via social media and the internet, and more. Compared to older generations, younger generations are more inclined to seek treatment and have open conversations about mental health. There is a growing trend toward mental health education in communities, businesses, and educational institutions. World Mental Health Day and Mental Health Awareness Month are two initiatives that offer forums for education and conversation. For people dealing with mental health concerns, social media efforts with hashtags like #MentalHealthMatters and #BreakTheStigma have aided in fostering a sense of support and community. There are still large knowledge and comprehension gaps in spite of this development. There are still misconceptions regarding mental health, and stigma is still a major obstacle. For instance, rather than seeing mental health disorders as real medical problems requiring appropriate treatment, many people still see them as a sign of moral failings or personal weakness. It is impossible to overestimate the influence of the media on how people see mental health. Negative or sensationalized portrayals of mental health issues can reinforce damaging stereotypes, whereas good portrayals can promote empathy and understanding. Representation in the media that is respectful and accurate is essential to eradicating stigma and promoting help-seeking behavior. With the goal of giving students the knowledge and abilities to manage their mental health and help their classmates, educational institutions have begun to include mental health curricula in their programs. In order to normalize mental health conversations and encourage early intervention, this is an essential first step. Additionally, companies are realizing the value of mental health and providing services to support their staff, such as mental health days and Employee Assistance Programs (EAPs).

Recent Change in Society and The effects They have on Mental Health

The fast-paced social transformation that the modern generation is experiencing has a significant impact on mental health. Anxiety and other mental health issues are on the rise as a result of several significant changes:

1. Technological Advancements and Social Media: The introduction of social media and the internet has completely changed how people interact and communicate. These platforms come with new obstacles in addition to their many advantages. Anxiety levels can rise as a result of feeling inadequate and having to offer an edited, idealized picture of oneself on social media. Cyberbullying and continual exposure to bad news aggravate these problems even more.The fear of missing out (FOMO) is a condition in which people worry about missing out on events they think others are enjoying. Social media can exacerbate this anxiety. This may result in excessive social media use and

compulsive checking, which could be detrimental to mental health.

2. Economic Uncertainty: A lot of young people live in precarious environments as a result of economic instability and increased living expenses. The high cost of housing, student loan debt, and job uncertainty all contribute to financial stress, which is a major cause of worry. In a competitive employment market, the pressure to achieve can result in mental health problems and burnout. A general sense of insecurity, as well as a large number of job losses and financial hardships, resulted from the global COVID-19 pandemic. Due to the fact that many people suffered elevated levels of anxiety, sadness, and other mental health difficulties during lockdowns and periods of social isolation, the pandemic also brought attention to the significance of mental health.

3. Cultural and Societal Pressures: Modern culture values success, productivity, and achievement highly. People may feel tremendous pressure to perform well in their academic endeavors, careers, and social lives as a result. Chronic tension and anxiety can result from the "hustle culture" and its emphasis on continuous work. In addition, social expectations about relationships, body image, and lifestyle choices can exacerbate mental health issues. Ads and the media's ubiquitous impact frequently propagate exaggerated notions of success and attractiveness, which breed feelings of inadequacy and low self-worth.

4. Environmental Concerns: Anxiety has grown in response to growing knowledge of environmental problems and climate change, especially in younger generations. Symptoms of this syndrome, called eco-anxiety, include helplessness, worry, and concern for the planet's future. An excessive sense of responsibility and

the need to address environmental issues might exacerbate mental health issues.

5. Social and Political Discontent: Differing political ideologies and social discontent have an effect on mental health as well. A sense of anxiety and tension might be brought on by the current socio-political milieu, which is marked by contentious language and widespread action. The continuous fight for justice and equality puts underprivileged people under additional stress and raises mental health issues.

6. Isolation and Loneliness: Many people report feeling alone and isolated, even though they are more connected than ever thanks to digital technologies. One factor contributing to this feeling of alienation is the breakdown of conventional social structures, including close-knit communities and extended family living arrangements. Depression and anxiety are among the mental health conditions for which loneliness is a substantial risk factor.

7. Health Crises and Pandemics: Epidemics, like the COVID-19 pandemic, have a significant impact on public health. The pandemic caused a great deal of anxiety, sadness, and uncertainty. Even though social distancing measures were required to stop the virus from spreading, they increased isolation and disturbed everyday routines. Strong mental health support services are necessary because the epidemic also revealed and made pre-existing mental health problems worse.

Handling the Crisis in Mental Health

A multifaceted approach is necessary in order to successfully address the mental health crisis facing the current generation. This comprises:

1. Improving Access to Mental Health Services: It's critical to make sure mental health services are both inexpensive and easily available. This entails offering low-cost or free mental health services, growing insurance coverage, and

boosting funding for mental health care. With the COVID-19 epidemic, telehealth services have grown in popularity and present a promising way to improve access to mental health care.

2. Encouraging Mental Health Education: Promoting mental health and lowering stigma both depend on education. By including mental health education in school curricula, youth can gain the knowledge and abilities necessary to take care of their mental health and assist their peers. Additionally important for lowering stigma and increasing awareness are workplace training initiatives and public health campaigns.

3. Building friendly communities: It's critical to create friendly environments where people feel comfortable talking about their mental health. This entails setting up online forums, peer support groups, and community mental health initiatives where people can talk about their experiences and get help. It can help normalize these discussions and lessen the fear of criticism

by promoting candid conversations about mental health.

4. Tackling Socio-Economic Inequalities: Resolving the underlying factors that contribute to economic stress and inequality can have a big effect on mental health. This involves promoting laws that offer financial stability, such as those that guarantee access to cheap housing, equitable pay, healthcare, and education. One way to mitigate the financial stress that leads to anxiety and other mental health problems is to reduce economic inequality.

5. Supporting Technology Use in a Healthy Way: Fostering technology and social media use in a healthy way can help lessen some of their detrimental effects on mental health. This includes fostering pleasant online relationships, establishing screen time limitations, and fostering digital literacy. It is imperative to provide resources and assistance to those who are victims of cyberbullying or online harassment.

6. Supporting Environmental and Social Justice Efforts: You may help reduce the anxiety that comes with environmental issues and social justice by supporting initiatives that aim to address them. This entails supporting neighborhood projects, advancing social justice, and lobbying for laws that address climate change. Giving people the tools to take action on these problems can also give them a feeling of agency and purpose, both of which are good for mental health.

7. Improving Mental Health Research: Funding for mental health research is necessary to provide interventions and therapies that work. This entails researching how cultural shifts affect mental health, investigating novel therapy modalities, and figuring out the best ways to provide mental health services.

Chapter 2

The Evolution of Mental Health Across the Ages

A Historical Analysis of the Origins of Stigmatization

It is essential to delve deeply into the historical background of stigmatization and its roots in order to comprehend the development of mental health. For ages, diverse cultural, religious, and philosophical ideas have influenced the way people see mental health concerns. This has resulted in the stigmatization and abuse of those who suffer from mental diseases.

Historical Societies Mental illness was frequently associated with supernatural forces or divine punishment in ancient civilizations. Historically, for example, people in Mesopotamia and Egypt thought that mental illnesses resulted from divine anger or demonic possession. During this time, the employment of herbs and potions meant to drive out bad spirits, exorcisms, and religious rites were common forms of treatment. In a similar vein, mental health was frequently associated with moral and spiritual deficiencies in classical Greece and Rome. Nonetheless, there were preliminary indications of more logical perspectives on mental health. Hippocrates, sometimes called the "Father of Medicine," postulated that abnormalities in body fluids, or "humors," were the root cause of mental illnesses. His support of lifestyle changes, physical activity, and rest helped pave the way for more compassionate methods of providing mental health services.

The Medieval Era Throughout the Middle Ages, the Church had a significant impact on how society viewed mental health. Many times, mental illness was seen as an indication of sin or demonic possession, which led to cruel therapies including whipping, exorcisms, and even executions. Social stigma and exclusion were commonplace for those who were considered mentally sick. Prehistoric times also saw the founding of the earliest asylums. These facilities, which frequently housed people with mental health disorders in appalling conditions, were more like jails than hospitals. Rather than treating them, the main goal was to keep them apart from society.

The Age of Enlightenment and the Renaissance A resurgence of interest in science and medicine during the Renaissance started to dispel preconceived notions and prejudices regarding mental health. Thinkers like William Tuke in England and Philippe Pinel in France developed more compassionate therapies for the mentally ill during the Enlightenment. Pinel was a well-known advocate for moral care that encompassed empathy, comprehension, and occupational therapy. He notably released inmates from chains in asylums in Paris. There was a dramatic change during the Age of Enlightenment from a moral or spiritual perspective on mental health issues to one of medicine. It was around this time that modern psychiatry began to take shape, and more methodical approaches to treatment emerged.

The Development of Treatment For Mental Health

The evolution of mental health care has been a difficult road filled with both successes and failures. Comprehending this progression aids in placing present procedures in perspective and emphasizes the significance of ongoing progress in the area.

Institutionalization and Reform in the 19th Century Asylums and mental hospitals proliferated throughout the 19th century, a sign of the rising realization that people with mental diseases need specialized treatment. But these facilities frequently overflowed and were underfunded, which resulted in subpar surroundings and treatment. Despite these difficulties, there were also important reforms during the 19th century. American mental health advocate Dorothea Dix pushed for improved care and the creation of state-run mental health facilities. Her work resulted in the establishment of almost thirty facilities devoted to mental health services. German psychiatrist Emil Kraepelin made significant contributions to the categorization of mental illnesses in Europe. He laid the foundation for contemporary psychiatric classification systems by emphasizing the value of methodical observation and diagnosis.

Psychopharmacology and Psychoanalysis in the Early 20th Century Psychoanalysis gained popularity in the early 20th century, thanks to Sigmund Freud's pioneering work. Freud's views on the unconscious mind and the significance of early life events in forming mental health had a significant influence on the area. With its emphasis on using talk therapy to unearth repressed memories and resolve internal conflicts, psychoanalysis rose to prominence as a therapeutic strategy. The development of psychopharmacology in the middle of the 20th century signaled a dramatic change. With the development of the first antipsychotic drug, chlorpromazine, in the 1950s, there was a new approach to treating the symptoms of serious mental diseases like schizophrenia. The introduction of anxiolytics and antidepressants during this time also helped millions of patients with mood and anxiety disorders.

Late 20th Century: Community Care and Deinstitutionalization The deinstitutionalization movement, which sought to relocate patients from major mental institutions to community-based care, was prominent in the second half of the 20th century. The availability of effective treatments, growing public awareness of the deplorable circumstances in asylums, and the fight for civil rights for those with mental diseases were some of the elements that propelled this movement. Deinstitutionalization brought with it substantial hurdles in addition to the goal of improving the quality of life for those with mental health issues. Underfunding and inadequate capacity to handle the requirements of individuals leaving institutions plagued many community-based programs, creating gaps in care and increasing the number of mentally ill people who became homeless or imprisoned.

Modern Methods: Integrated and Comprehensive Healthcare A more comprehensive and holistic approach is what defines mental health care today. The biological, psychological, and social aspects that contribute to mental health problems are now well understood, thanks to developments in neuroscience, psychology, and medication. This has made it possible to provide more individualized and efficient care. For a variety of mental health issues, dialectical behavior therapy (DBT), cognitive-behavioral therapy (CBT), and other evidence-based psychotherapies are now considered standard treatments. These therapies give patients useful skills to manage their symptoms by focusing on altering maladaptive thought patterns and actions. Treatment accessibility has also increased as a result of the integration of mental health services into primary care settings. Empirical evidence suggests that collaborative care models involving mental health specialists, primary care doctors, and other healthcare professionals lead to better results for patients with mental health disorders. Furthermore, the significance of tackling socioeconomic determinants of health, like housing, work, and social support, in fostering mental well-being is becoming increasingly evident. A growing number of people are adopting holistic methods that take into account an individual's entire being, including their lifestyle, social surroundings, and physical health.

Change In Attitude over time

Over the ages, societal perceptions of mental health have changed dramatically. There have been noticeable movements in the direction of more acceptance and understanding, even while stigma and misconceptions still exist.

Early Fear and Stigmatization In the past, stigma around mental illness was common in the ancient and medieval periods. There was a great deal of shame associated with the idea that moral shortcomings or supernatural forces were to blame for mental illnesses. It was common for those with mental health problems to face discrimination, persecution, or cruel treatment. Ineffective treatments and a lack of knowledge contributed to the early stigmatization. Negative myths and prejudices persisted in part because of the lack of scientific understanding regarding the brain and mental health.

Early Reforms and the Enlightenment

The Enlightenment era signaled a shift in public perceptions of mental health. As the demand for compassion and understanding grew, new humane treatment modalities like moral therapy emerged. During this time, the idea that mental illness is a moral flaw started to give way to the idea that it is a physical problem. However, stigma persisted despite these developments. The persistence of asylum usage and the marginalization of those suffering from mental health disorders brought to light the continuous difficulties in bringing about a change in societal attitudes.

20th Century: Advancements and Reversals Public awareness and mental health care have advanced significantly in the 20th century. The emergence of psychoanalysis and the discovery of psychotropic drugs offered fresh perspectives on the causes and treatments of mental health issues. The goal of the deinstitutionalization movement was to reintegrate people with mental health disorders into society, signifying a change in attitude toward their rights and increased inclusion. There were obstacles throughout this time, though. Though well-intentioned, the deinstitutionalization movement frequently lacked the resources and support needed to deliver quality community-based care. As a result, people with mental health concerns began to contact the criminal justice system more frequently and faced new difficulties, such as homelessness.

Modern Views: Raising Knowledge and Campaigning The last few decades have witnessed a notable surge in the recognition and promotion of mental health. The impact of social media, public health initiatives, and mental health advocates' work has opened up the conversation regarding mental health concerns. The stigma associated with mental health is gradually fading, especially among younger people. Compared to other generations, millennials and Generation Z are more inclined to seek treatment and have open conversations about mental health. The growing number of programs focused on enhancing mental well-being and the rising demand for mental health services both reflect this transition. It is impossible to overestimate the influence of popular culture and the media on how people see mental health. Speaking out about their challenges with mental health, celebrities and public figures have contributed to normalizing these disorders and lowering stigma. Accurate and sympathetic representations of mental health challenges in literature, film, and television have also contributed to the development of better empathy and understanding.

Continued Difficulties and Future Prospects
Even with the advancements, there are still big obstacles in the way of altering society's perceptions of mental health. Stigma still exists in numerous forms, one of which is self-stigma, which occurs when people internalize self-defeating thoughts. For many people with mental health concerns, discrimination persists as a barrier in the workplace, educational institutions, and healthcare settings. Continued campaigns to advance mental health education, lessen stigma, and support mental health-promoting policies are required to solve these issues. To enhance mental well-being, it is imperative to allocate more funds for mental health services, include mental health in wider healthcare systems, and tackle the social determinants of health that affect mental health. Furthermore, more study is required to determine the origins and remedies of mental health issues. Developments in psychology, genetics, and neuroscience could lead to the creation of more individualized and efficient therapies. We can keep combating stigma and

enhancing the lives of those who suffer from mental illnesses by promoting a greater knowledge of mental health.

Chapter 3

Societal Attitudes and Their Impact

The media has long been crucial in influencing how society views a range of topics, including mental health. Media portrayals of mental health have a tremendous impact on public image and stigma, ranging from news articles and television shows to films and television shows.

Historical Representations

In the past, the media has frequently sensationalized and presented mental health in a negative light. The portrayal of people with mental health disorders in early movies and TV series was usually one of violence, instability, and danger. These representations contributed to the dread and misunderstanding that pervaded society and reinforced negative prejudices. For instance, mental health characters in great movies like "Psycho" (1960) and "One Flew Over the Cuckoo's Nest" (1975) were either violent mental health system victims or murderous maniacs. These representations served to perpetuate the notion that individuals with mental health issues should be pitied or feared rather than understood and helped. Development and accurate representation The media has been gradually moving in the direction of more truthful and sympathetic representations of mental health in recent years. This shift is indicative of a larger social shift in favor of increased understanding and acceptance of mental health concerns. Television programs such as "13 Reasons Why" and "BoJack Horseman" have sensitively and nuancedly addressed difficult mental health issues, igniting vital dialogues among viewers. Destigmatizing mental health has also benefited from reality TV and documentaries. Real people discussing their personal experiences with mental health issues humanize the problem and offer a more grounded viewpoint in programs like this one. These narratives have the power to increase empathy and compassion in viewers by presenting mental health issues as a natural part of life.

The Impact of the Media on the Need for Assistance

The way the media presents mental health can have a big influence on people's willingness to ask for assistance. Positive portrayals that highlight characters getting care and support can inspire viewers to ask for assistance on their own. On the other hand, inaccurate representations that paint mental health treatments as detrimental or ineffectual may deter individuals from getting the therapy they require. Public service announcements (PSAs) and campaigns in the media have also been essential in raising awareness of mental health issues. Efforts to lessen stigma and promote candid conversations about mental health include "Time to Change" in the UK and "Make It OK" in the US. These campaigns make use of media channels to enlighten the public, disseminate encouraging words, and offer resources to those in need of assistance.

Cultural Differences in Mental Health Stigma

Cultural Variations in the Shame of Mental Illness Cultural values and ideas have a major role in shaping attitudes toward mental health and the stigma attached to mental illness. For the purpose of creating efficient mental health interventions and advancing global mental health fairness, it is imperative to comprehend these cultural variations.

Non-Western and Western Views

The acceptance of mental health disorders as real medical diseases requiring treatment is spreading in many Western nations. But stigma still endures, frequently stemming from fear and misunderstandings. Western societies tend to place a strong emphasis on individualism, which might focus attention on personal accountability for mental health. This viewpoint occasionally makes self-stigma worse, as people hold themselves responsible for their mental health issues. Non-Western cultures, on the other hand, might have distinct perspectives on mental health. For instance, strong cultural ideals surrounding societal peace and family honor frequently stigmatize mental health concerns in many Asian societies. Reluctance to seek treatment and underreporting of mental health issues might result from the perception that admitting to a problem will bring shame to the family. Conventional wisdom regarding mental health, such as the existence of spirits or karma, can also impact treatment philosophies and patient perspectives.

Native American and Minority Groups Indigenous and minority groups frequently have particular difficulties because of the stigma associated with mental illness. Racial prejudice, societal injustices, and historical trauma all contribute to increased rates of mental health problems and care-seeking obstacles. Moreover, a cultural mistrust of Western medical systems may prevent people from seeking assistance. Indigenous communities, for example, might favor traditional healing methods over modern mental health care. Including cultural customs and beliefs in mental health treatment can increase its efficacy and acceptance. Community-based strategies that include members of the community and family in the healing process can also be advantageous.

The Significance of Spirituality and Religion The influence of religion and spirituality on cultural attitudes towards mental health is noteworthy. A number of religious perspectives see mental health disorders as spiritual crises or challenges to one's faith. This viewpoint can be stigmatizing as well as supportive. Religious groups can, on the one hand, offer robust social support systems that aid in mental health. However, stigmatization and discouragement from seeking professional assistance might result from the conviction that mental health issues are the result of a lack of faith or moral failure.

The Impact of Social Media and Online Communities

There are many ways in which social media and online groups have changed the mental health landscape, both positively and negatively. In order to maximize the advantages of digital platforms while reducing their risks, it is imperative to comprehend their effects.

Beneficial Affects Social media has made mental health conversations more accessible by giving people a forum to share their stories, look for help, and get information. People who feel alone or stigmatized might find great value in the sense of belonging and validation that online communities and support groups provide. Utilizing the power of social media, campaigns and movements like #BellLetsTalk and #MentalHealthAwareness have reduced stigma and raised awareness. These programs support mental health activism, facilitate resource sharing for education, and foster candid communication. These discussions have become more commonplace as a result of influencers and celebrities using their platforms to talk about their personal difficulties with mental health. Social media can make it easier to obtain resources and services related to mental health. To disseminate mental health information, offer online treatment services, and conduct psychoeducation, numerous organizations and mental health practitioners use social media. More and more people are using telehealth to get mental health care, especially those who might otherwise face obstacles to getting treatment—especially in the wake of the COVID-19 outbreak.

Adverse Effects Social media has advantages, but it can also have drawbacks for mental health. Constant exposure to idealized lives and pictures can cause anxiety, low self-esteem, and feelings of inadequacy. People may experience worsening emotions due to the "FOMO" phenomenon, which occurs when they contrast their lives with those of others who appear to have flawless lives. Online harassment and cyberbullying are serious issues, especially for youth. Cyberbullying victims are more likely to experience mental health problems like anxiety, depression, and suicidal thoughts. People may be more inclined to participate in dangerous behaviors on the internet due to their anonymity than they could be in person. Social media's addictive qualities may potentially be a factor in mental health issues. Overuse of social media has been associated with disturbed sleep, elevated stress levels, and reduced physical activity, all of which can have detrimental effects on mental well-being. Burnout and social media weariness are further consequences of the obligation to continuously interact and maintain an online presence.

The Function of Echo Chambers and Algorithms Because social media algorithms are meant to increase user interaction, they have the potential to produce echo chambers, where people are mostly exposed to information that confirms their own opinions. Although this can foster a feeling of belonging and validation, it can also spread false information and stigma around mental health. For instance, people who interact with content that stigmatizes mental health may discover that a torrent of similar content appears in their feeds, which perpetuates unfavorable attitudes and false beliefs. On the other hand, those who are looking for knowledge about constructive coping mechanisms and mental health therapies can profit from tailored content that promotes their wellbeing.

Innovations and digital interventions New, novel mental health solutions have also become more prevalent in the digital age. As effective tools for managing mental health, smartphone apps that provide mindfulness, meditation, cognitive-behavioral therapy (CBT) activities, and mood tracking have gained popularity. These apps offer affordable and easily accessible means for people to receive mental health care, especially for those who might find traditional therapy unsuitable. Emerging technologies like artificial intelligence (AI) and virtual reality (VR) may have uses in the field of mental health. VR offers a safe space for people to face their concerns, making it a useful tool in the treatment of anxiety and post-traumatic stress disorder (PTSD). AI-powered chatbots provide a different way for those in need of mental health help by giving them access to information and prompt responses.

Final Thoughts A complex mix of media influences, cultural beliefs, and technological developments shapes societal views about mental health. Even though there has been a lot of progress in raising awareness and decreasing stigma, there are still obstacles to overcome in order to provide fair access to mental health services and create supportive environments for those who are struggling with mental health concerns. Public opinions are greatly influenced by the media, and positive change can be fostered by utilizing its power. Reduced stigma and increased help-seeking behavior can result from truthful and compassionate representations of mental health in movies, TV shows, and the news. However, in order to safeguard mental health, it is crucial to address the detrimental effects of social media, such as cyberbullying and the temptation to project an idealized image of oneself. Cultural differences in perspectives on mental health emphasize the need for care delivery methods that are sensitive to cultural differences. Acknowledging and honoring a range of viewpoints can enhance the efficacy of mental health interventions and advance equity in mental health worldwide. The emergence of social media and virtual communities has brought up both novel prospects and obstacles concerning mental well-being. Fostering a healthy digital environment requires balancing the negative effects of digital platforms with their positives, such as easier access to services and help. Sustaining mental health will require constant education, advocacy, and innovation in the area as society changes. Only then will mental health become a valued and supported aspect of the world. We can strive toward a future in which mental health is given the consideration, respect, and care it merits by comprehending and tackling the many variables that shape society's attitudes.

Chapter 4

The Intersection of Stigma and Anxiety

Anxiety disorders, one of the most prevalent mental health issues, impact millions of individuals globally. Anxiety is a complex condition with many underlying causes, including biological, psychological, genetic, and environmental variables. However, the stigma surrounding mental health issues makes anxiety worse. Stigma can create a vicious cycle in which experiences of discrimination and exclusion on a personal level, as well as cultural views, can make people more anxious.

The Character of Shame

Stigma refers to unfavorable attitudes, convictions, and actions against someone based on specific traits—in this case, mental health disorders. Stigma comes in a variety of forms, such as: **Public Stigma**: Negative perceptions of people with mental health disorders in society. **Self-Stigma**: An internalized sense of guilt and disgrace that people with mental illnesses go through. Structural Stigma: Discriminatory systemic policies and practices directed towards people with mental health disorders. People who suffer from anxiety and other mental health disorders may feel isolated and unsupported in this atmosphere, which can exacerbate their symptoms considerably. This is because stigma takes many different forms.

Shame and the Apprehension of Appraisal

The dread of judgment is one of the main ways that stigma increases anxiety. Anxious people frequently worry excessively about what other people think of them. These anxieties become more intense when society has stigmatizing beliefs about mental health. Worrying about being called "weak," "unstable," or "crazy" might make people more anxious in social settings because they are more likely to feel exposed and judged. A person who suffers from social anxiety, for instance, could steer clear of professional meetings or social events out of concern that others would notice and criticize them. Although this avoidance strategy offers short-term respite, over time it perpetuates the anxiety by keeping the person from confronting and conquering their anxieties in a supportive setting.

Shame and the Reluctance to Ask for Assistance Stigma also affects people's willingness to get anxiety treatment. People may be reluctant to seek help from mental health specialists out of fear of stigma, which can result in anxiety that is untreated or poorly controlled. This resistance to asking for assistance is especially noticeable in societies where there is a strong stigma associated with mental health and when doing so is viewed as a sign of weakness or failure. Severe symptoms and coexisting disorders like depression might result from untreated anxiety. In addition, a lack of assistance and efficient care can cause serious impairments in day-to-day functioning that impact relationships, productivity at work, and general quality of life.

Social isolation and stigma

The experience of stigma frequently results in social isolation, which is a major cause of anxiety. People who experience stigmatization may distance themselves from social situations in order to prevent prejudice and unfavorable comments. They may miss out on the social connections and support that are essential for mental health as a result of their isolation. There is a substantial correlation between social isolation, loneliness, and elevated anxiety. Anxiety symptoms might get worse in response to a lack of social interaction and support, which can heighten pessimism and feelings of powerlessness. As a result, it is critical to remove stigma in order to promote inclusive and supportive societies. On the other hand, supportive relationships and positive social interactions are known to have a protective impact on anxiety.

Case Studies: Personal Stories of Struggle and Resilience

Individual Narratives of Adversity and Fortitude Gaining insight into the effects of anxiety stigma through firsthand accounts can help one develop a more compassionate and profound understanding of the problem. The following case studies highlight the hardships and resiliency of those who have experienced stigma because of their anxiety.

Example 1: Emily's Experience with Social Anxiety Since she was a teenager, 28-year-old Emily, a marketing professional, has battled social anxiety. In her small-town upbringing, Emily accepted the notion that her worry was a personal shortcoming. Because she was afraid people would see her trembling hands and hear her unsteady voice, she shied away from social gatherings and public speaking. Emily's anxiety increased while she was in college, but she was too ashamed to get treatment. Because of the stigma in her society around mental health, she was afraid that going to treatment would make her look "mad." Emily didn't start talking openly about her difficulties until she relocated to a bigger city and formed a group of encouraging friends. With the support of her friends, Emily went to treatment and received a social anxiety disorder diagnosis. She was able to control her anxiety by using gradual exposure approaches and cognitive-behavioral treatment (CBT). In addition, Emily developed into a mental health awareness activist, using her personal experience to encourage others who might be suffering in silence. Many in her community have found inspiration in her tenacity and willingness to ask for assistance in spite of the stigma.

Case Study No. 2: Raj's Struggle with Anxiety Raj, an IT specialist of 35 years, had his first panic episode when he was just a young man. He was scared when he suddenly experienced extreme panic, palpitations in his heart, and dyspnea. Raj misinterpreted his symptoms and believed he was suffering a heart attack. After numerous trips to the emergency department without any physical cause, panic disorder was diagnosed. Raj's family disregarded his illness, viewing it as nothing more than "nervousness" that he needed to manage on his own, due to ingrained cultural ideas that stigmatized mental health. Raj attempted to conceal his panic episodes out of shame and a lack of support, which made him feel even more anxious. Raj joined an online support group for people with panic disorder after years of suffering in silence. His discovery of understanding and common experiences within the group marked a sea change for him. He came to understand that getting expert assistance was not a sign of weakness and that he wasn't alone. Raj started therapy and was able to properly manage his panic problem with the help of his online network. His narrative emphasizes how crucial support networks and communities are to overcoming stigma and developing resilience. Case Study

Case study 3: Generalized Anxiety Disorder (GAD) Struggle for Maria Maria, a 42-year-old educator, has spent the majority of her life dealing with generalized anxiety disorder (GAD). Maria struggled to unwind because she was always thinking about many parts of her life, such as her health and her performance at work. Being a mental health professional, she was reluctant to report her ailment due to the stigma surrounding mental health disorders. When Maria took on more duties at work, her anxiety got worse. She started to have physical symptoms, such as persistent headaches and sleeplessness, but she believed that getting help or taking a break would make her appear weak. Burnout resulted from her refusal to treat her anxiety due to fear of social disapproval. Maria eventually confided in a reliable coworker, who urged her to give her mental health first priority. Maria managed to control her GAD with the assistance of a specialist and workplace modifications. Additionally, she began promoting mental health awareness at her school, fostering a more encouraging atmosphere for both teachers and kids. Maria's fortitude in the face of stigma emphasizes the transformational potential of advocacy and support for oneself.

The Psychological Impact of Being Stigmatized

The psychological effects of stigma on people who experience anxiety are extensive and complex. In addition to making anxiety symptoms worse, stigma has an impact on identity, self-worth, and general mental health, among other areas of psychological well-being.

Self-worth and self-esteem The effects of stigma on a person's sense of worth and self-esteem can be profound. People who suffer from anxiety may adopt unfavorable attitudes about mental health disorders from society, which can result in feelings of inferiority and humiliation. Internalized stigma might appear as self-deprecating ideas like "I am a burden" or "I am weak." Anxiety can persist and worsen as a result of low self-worth and esteem. People may experience an excessive amount of self-consciousness and hypervigilance regarding their perceived imperfections, which can exacerbate their anxiety in social and performance contexts. Their skewed view of themselves may also make them reluctant to ask for assistance since they may believe they are not deserving of it or that they are incapable of getting better. Self-Awareness and Identity Furthermore, stigma impacts a person's sense of identity and self-concept. Anxiety sufferers may come to identify with their illness, making their identity entwined with their mental health issues. They may see themselves and their future through a narrow lens due to their stigmatized identity, which limits their sense of their strengths and potential. A fractured sense of self might result from the pressure to hide one's anxieties and live up to social norms. People may exhibit masking behaviors, putting on a front of wellbeing while going through internal struggles. Feelings of inauthenticity and unhappiness may result from this discrepancy between their presentation on the outside and their inside experience.

Comorbidities and Mental Health Stigma's psychological effects go beyond fear; it also plays a role in the emergence of co-occurring mental health disorders. Depression, substance misuse, and other mental health problems can result from the stress and isolation brought on by stigma. For instance, persistent anxiety over criticism and rejection can lead to depressive symptoms including worthlessness, sadness, and disinterest in activities. Some people who bear the combined burden of stigma and anxiety may turn to substance misuse as a coping method. While self-medicating with alcohol or drugs can momentarily reduce anxiety symptoms, doing so eventually causes more issues with both mental and physical health.

Interpersonal and social relationships Stigma has an impact on interpersonal and social interactions, making it more difficult to establish and preserve supportive relationships. Fear of criticism or misunderstanding is a common reason why people with anxiety avoid social situations. This social disengagement might worsen anxiety symptoms and result in loneliness. Relationship pressure might also result from stigma. People with stigmatizing beliefs—friends, family, and coworkers—may be less supportive of the person experiencing anxiety or react badly to it. This lack of comprehension and empathy can result in disagreements, a decline in social support, and a rise in loneliness. On the other hand, strong social support can mitigate the damaging effects of stigma. In order to manage anxiety and improve wellbeing, supportive connections offer a sense of belonging, practical help, and emotional validation. Fostering a frank and transparent dialogue around mental health can improve bonds between people and lessen the negative impacts of stigma.

Techniques for Lowering Stigma and Assisting People Who Are Anxious In order to effectively address the relationship between stigma and anxiety, comprehensive solutions involving advocacy, education.

Chapter 5

Encouraging Help-Seeking Behavior

Barriers to Seeking Help

Obstacles to Asking for Assistance Many obstacles still stand in the way of people seeking treatment for anxiety and other mental health illnesses, even in spite of the increased public awareness of mental health issues. These obstacles are complex, involving systemic, cultural, personal, and financial elements.

Psychological and Personal Barriers

1. Shame and stigma: The stigma around mental health is one of the biggest individual obstacles. Many people are afraid that if they admit to having anxiety, they will be mistreated, branded,

or subjected to discrimination. They may feel ashamed and embarrassed as a result of this fear, which keeps them from getting the assistance they require.

2. Denial and Minimization: Some people may choose to downplay or reject their symptoms because they don't think they're severe enough to need medical attention. Individuals may believe that self-management is sufficient, failing to acknowledge that anxiety disorders are serious medical problems requiring medical attention.

3. Fear of therapy: Another barrier may be fear of the actual therapy procedure. Some people might be afraid of the adverse effects or worried about the stigma associated with taking medicine. Some people may be afraid of therapy because they think it will include awkward or painful talks.

4. Lack of Awareness: People may refrain from getting treatment if they are unaware of mental health issues and their options. They might not be aware of the supports and services that are

available to them, or they might not realize that their symptoms are suggestive of an anxiety problem.

Social and Cultural Barriers

1. **Cultural Beliefs and Norms:** How people approach mental health depends a lot on their culture. A lack of spiritual faith or a show of personal weakness are two cultural perceptions associated with mental health concerns. These cultural preconceptions have the power to compound stigma and deter people from getting treatment.

2. **Family and Community Dynamics**: Barriers may also arise from the impact of family and community. In close-knit groups, people may conceal their difficulties out of fear of rumors or criticism from others. Those with stigmatizing beliefs about mental health within the family may put off getting professional assistance even more.

3. **Social Isolation:** It may be more difficult for someone to ask for assistance if they are socially isolated or do not have supportive relationships. If friends and family don't support or encourage them, they may feel alone in their troubles and be less inclined to ask for help.

Economic and systemic barriers

1. **Availability and Accessibility:** The scarcity of readily available and easily accessible mental health services is a major systemic obstacle. A lack of mental health providers and facilities may exist in many places, especially in underserved or rural communities. Long wait times and obstacles to receiving care may discourage people from asking for assistance.

2. **Cost and Insurance:** For many people, the expense of receiving mental health care is unaffordable. People might not be able to afford counseling, medicine, or other treatments if they don't have enough insurance or money. Two of the biggest obstacles to receiving mental health

services are high out-of-pocket expenses and inadequate insurance coverage.

3. **Work and Time Constraints**: Realistic factors like work schedules and time restraints might sometimes discourage people from asking for assistance. It might be difficult to find time for appointments, especially during business hours. Employers who do not offer sufficient leave policies or mental health help may make this problem more difficult to handle.

4. **Lack of Trust in the System**: People may be discouraged from seeking treatment if they have had bad experiences with mental health services in the past, have privacy concerns, or lack faith in the healthcare system. Individuals who have encountered prejudice or substandard treatment can be hesitant to utilize mental health resources once more.

Strategies to Reduce Stigma and Promote Awareness

Developing all-encompassing initiatives to lessen stigma and raise mental health awareness is necessary to address the obstacles to getting care. Public education, community involvement, policy reforms, and individual and family empowerment are some of these tactics.

Campaigns for Public Education

1. Raising Awareness: By increasing public knowledge of anxiety and other mental health concerns, public education efforts can lessen stigma and help normalize these problems. Campaigns should emphasize that anxiety is a widespread and treatable disorder by accurately describing its symptoms, causes, and remedies.

2. Challenge Misconceptions: One goal of education should be to dispel myths that people have about mental health. Campaigns, for instance, can target the misconception that anxiety is only a result of one's own weakness or that willpower is sufficient to conquer it. Depicting individual accounts of recuperation

and resiliency can aid in dispelling these misconceptions.

3. Encouraging Positive Messaging: It's critical to promote help-seeking behavior through positive messaging. Ads must highlight the positive effects of treatment—like an enhanced quality of life—and offer information on where to get support. Self-care and highlighting the fact that asking for assistance is a sign of strength can help shift unfavorable beliefs.

Community involvement and assistance

1.Grassroots efforts: In order to lessen stigma and raise awareness of mental health issues, community-based efforts can be extremely important. Individuals and families can get education, resources, and support from neighborhood organizations, support groups, and advocacy networks. Engagement with the community should be based on the needs of the community and attentive to cultural differences.

2. Peer Support: Programs where people who have personally experienced anxiety offer guidance and support to one another can be quite successful. Peer supporters can make people feel understood and less alone by providing them with empathy, motivation, and useful guidance. Additionally, these programs might act as a link to in-person therapy.

3. Workplace Mental Health Programs: By putting in place workplace mental health programs, employers can help lessen stigma. Work-life balance and mental health policy, as well as counseling service accessibility and education, should all be part of these programs. Fostering a positive work atmosphere helps motivate staff to ask for assistance when necessary.

Advocacy and Policy Changes

1. Improving Access to Care: It is imperative to make policy changes targeted at enhancing mental health care accessibility. This entails boosting insurance coverage for mental health

care, addressing labor shortages in the mental health industry, and raising funding for mental health services. Enhancing access through policies that facilitate telehealth and remote care is particularly beneficial in underprivileged communities. Enforcing and fortifying anti-discrimination legislation that safeguards people with mental health disorders can lessen stigma and encourage people to seek care. Legal safeguards can aid in preventing discrimination against people based on their mental health state in the workplace, the classroom, and other spheres of life.

3. Public Policy and Advocacy: In order to bring about systemic change, advocacy is essential. Advocates for mental health can seek to organize resources, change public policy, and increase public understanding. Advocacy organizations, medical professionals, and legislators working together can result in more comprehensive and successful mental health programs.

Strengthening Families and Individuals

1. Education and Empowerment: Giving people the information they need to make educated decisions about their care will help them become more knowledgeable about mental health. Educating people about anxiety, available treatments, and self-help techniques can empower them to actively manage their mental health.

2. Family Involvement: It might be helpful to include family in mental health education and support. Families can be extremely important in promoting help-seeking behavior and offering continuous assistance. It is possible to lessen stigma within the family and foster a more supportive atmosphere by teaching family members about anxiety and how to support their loved ones.

3. Building Resilience: A crucial component of mental wellness is resilience building. People can manage their anxiety more effectively and lessen the negative effects of stigma by

participating in programs and therapies that support emotional regulation, stress management, and coping skills. Programs for the community, businesses, and educational institutions can all incorporate resilience training.

Role of Education and Advocacy

In order to lessen stigma and encourage help-seeking behavior for anxiety and other mental health issues, advocacy and education are essential. These initiatives may result in a society that is more knowledgeable, sympathetic, and encouraging.

School-Based Mental Health Education

1. Integrating Mental Health into Curricula: Educational institutions have a significant influence on how people see mental health. By including mental health education in the curriculum, schools may give their pupils the

skills and information they need to comprehend and take care of their mental health. It should cover subjects including managing stress, controlling emotions, and identifying anxiety symptoms.

2. Educator Training: To effectively serve kids with mental health problems, educators must get training. Programs for professional development should give educators the skills and information they need to identify and address anxiety and other mental health concerns. Psychologists and counselors are examples of mental health specialists who have to be on hand in schools to offer assistance.

3. Building a Supportive School Environment: Schools ought to cultivate an atmosphere that encourages mental health. This entails putting anti-bullying measures into place, making mental health resources accessible, and promoting candid discussions about mental health. By fostering an environment of support and inclusion, we can lessen stigma and motivate kids to ask for assistance.

Campaigns for Public Health and Media Advocacy

1. Using Media Platforms: Media outlets can be effective instruments for advocating for mental health. Public health campaigns can reach a large audience and disseminate positive messages about mental health by utilizing social media, radio, television, and other media platforms. Testimonials, instructional materials, and details on where to get assistance should all be part of these initiatives.

2. Partnering with Influencers: You can spread awareness of mental health issues by working with prominent personalities and influencers who have a sizable fan base. Open discussions about their personal experiences with anxiety by celebrities and social media influencers can help normalize mental health issues and lessen stigma. They can encourage help-seeking

behavior and raise awareness of mental health issues by using their platforms.

3. Encouraging Mental Health Literacy: The goal of public health initiatives should be to raise mental health literacy, or the understanding and knowledge of mental health issues and treatments. People who have higher mental health literacy are better able to identify symptoms, get the right care, and support others. Campaigns ought to offer understandable, easily obtainable information that deconstructs mental health conditions.

Conclusion

The Widespread Effect of Stigma Numerous people who suffer from anxiety and other mental health illnesses are impacted by the pervasive stigma around mental health issues in society. Stigma can take many different forms, such as structural, self-, and public stigma, all of which add to a complicated web of problems that impede the wellbeing of people who are impacted by it. Public stigma refers to attitudes and ideas in society that diminish the worth of those who have mental health problems, resulting in exclusion and discrimination. When people internalize these negative beliefs, it can lead to feelings of shame and inadequacy, which is known as self-stigma. Policies and practices that restrict access to treatment and support are ingrained with structural stigma, which exacerbates systemic injustices.

The Way in Which Stigma Boosts Anxiety

Anxiety and stigma have a reciprocal, self-sustaining relationship. Stigma increases anxiety by creating a climate of distrust and condemnation. Anxious people frequently worry about what other people think of them, which makes them more anxious in social settings. People may hide their symptoms and put off getting care out of fear of being classified as "weak" or "unstable." One of the most detrimental repercussions of stigma is the unwillingness to ask for assistance. People may put off or refuse therapy out of fear of prejudice and judgment, which makes their anxiety worse. Untreated anxiety can negatively impact relationships, cause significant impairments in day-to-day functioning, and hasten the onset of other mental health conditions like depression.

The Shift in Perceptions About Mental Health

The way that society views mental health has changed over time and is a reflection of larger historical, social, and cultural changes. The past saw mental health problems as morally reprehensible or subject to supernatural power, which led to stigmatization and misunderstanding. The basic and frequently cruel treatment methods demonstrated a lack of comprehension and humanity. Our knowledge of mental health issues has improved over time as a result of developments in psychology and medicine. The emergence of efficacious therapies, such as medication and psychotherapy, has opened up new approaches to anxiety management. Notwithstanding these developments, stigma endures because of societal standards, media representations, and cultural attitudes.

The media's function and cultural disparities

The media has a big impact on how people see mental health. Even though honest and compassionate representations of mental health concerns have improved, sensationalized and stigmatizing depictions still contribute to unfavorable opinions. The portrayal of anxious people as "mad" or "dangerous" feeds negative preconceptions and deters people from getting help. Cultural variations are also a major factor in the ways that stigma around mental health issues appears. Certain societies severely stigmatize mental health problems, considering them a cause of embarrassment or an indication of one's own shortcomings. These cultural beliefs may erect further obstacles in the way of people asking for assistance and support, which makes it even harder for them to get the care they require.

Online Communities, Social Media and The Challenges

The growth of social media and online forums has affected the stigma associated with mental illness in both positive and negative ways. Positively, internet platforms give people a place to talk about their experiences, get support, and learn about mental health. For those who struggle with anxiety, online groups can help them feel less alone and more like they belong.

Social media, though, can often make stigma and anxiety worse. The dissemination of false information, the need to project an idealized image, and the worry about cyberbullying can all lead to increased anxiety and reinforce unfavorable preconceptions. It's critical to weigh the advantages and disadvantages of social media in order to support mental health and lessen stigma.

Individual Narratives and Fortitude

Narratives of personal struggles and perseverance underscore the significant influence of stigma on people who suffer from anxiety. Case studies of people such as Emily, Raj, and Maria highlight the various ways in which stigma influences behavior related to seeking treatment, self-worth, and general well-being. These tales highlight how crucial advocacy, comprehension, and support are to eradicating stigma. Maria's battle with generalized anxiety disorder, Raj's battle with panic disorder, and Emily's journey with social anxiety all serve as examples of the transformational potential of receiving help. These people overcame tremendous obstacles and stigma to learn how to control their anxiety, promote mental health awareness, and help others going through similar experiences.

Resolving Obstacles to Requesting Assistance
Encouraging help-seeking behavior requires addressing the different obstacles people encounter. Awareness and education efforts that normalize mental health issues and encourage positive attitudes might help to lessen psychological and personal barriers like stigma, denial, and treatment-related dread. Targeted treatments that respect and address cultural ideas and community dynamics are necessary to overcome social and cultural barriers. The implementation of peer support programs, community participation, and family involvement are crucial tactics in fostering supportive environments that promote

help-seeking behavior. Advocacy and policy reforms are necessary in response to systemic and economic impediments, such as lack of access to care, cost, and employment constraints. Reducing these obstacles requires instituting workplace mental health initiatives, increasing insurance coverage, and improving access to mental health care.

Techniques for Raising Awareness and Reducing Stigma

Reducing stigma and raising awareness of mental health issues necessitate a multimodal strategy that includes community involvement, public education, policy reforms, and personal empowerment.

1. Public Education Campaigns**: These should dispel myths, offer factual information on anxiety and other mental health issues, and encourage the practice of seeking treatment when necessary. It can help mainstream mental health issues and lessen stigma by highlighting human tales and recovery narratives.

2. Community Engagement and Support: Peer support groups, workplace mental health programs, and grassroots campaigns can all help create friendly environments and lessen stigma in the community. Effective engagement requires culturally sensitive methods and the participation of community leaders.

3. Policy Reforms and Advocacy: Access to care, the application of anti-discrimination legislation, and the promotion of telehealth are among areas where policy reforms can help lower systemic obstacles. In order to promote mental health programs, influence policy, and gather funding, advocacy groups are essential.

4. Empowering Individuals and Families: Empowerment and education can assist people in making knowledgeable decisions regarding their mental health treatment. For those who suffer from anxiety, family participation and the development of resilience via coping mechanisms and stress management techniques can be extremely helpful.

The Significance of Education to Protest The main components of the campaign to lessen stigma and promote help-seeking behavior are advocacy and education. To change attitudes and increase awareness, public health initiatives, media campaigns, and mental health education in schools are essential. In order to successfully support pupils, schools should train their teachers in mental health education and incorporate it into their curricula. In order to reach a large audience, advance mental health literacy, and foster good attitudes toward mental health, public health initiatives should make use of a variety of media outlets. It is possible to spread these messages and reach a larger audience by collaborating with public figures and influencers. Advocacy groups need to keep pushing for legislative improvements that will increase access to care and shield those who suffer from mental illnesses from prejudice. To create a society that is more welcoming and inclusive, advocates, legislators, and healthcare professionals must work together.

Going Ahead: An Appeal for Participation The effort to lessen the stigma associated with mental health problems and to promote help-seeking behavior is a continuous one. Everyone must work together—individuals, communities, healthcare professionals, legislators, and activists. We can create a society where people with anxiety and other mental health disorders feel empowered to seek the care they need by addressing the various obstacles to getting the help they need and fostering a culture of acceptance and support.

1. Building Empathy and Understanding: A key component of lowering stigma is building empathy and understanding. We need to keep spreading awareness about mental health issues, confronting our prejudices, and offering help to those in need.

2. Supporting mental health programs: It's important to support mental health programs through advocacy, contributions, or volunteer

work. These programs offer vital tools, assistance, and knowledge that can significantly improve the lives of those who struggle with anxiety.

3. Encouraging Open Conversations: We can help mainstream these challenges and lessen stigma by promoting open dialogue about mental health in both our personal and professional lives. Establishing safe areas for conversation helps promote a welcoming and encouraging atmosphere.

4. Advocating for Policy Change: It is crucial to advocate for changes to policies that enhance care access, safeguard people with mental health issues, and advance mental health education. Systemic changes that are advantageous to all parties can result from interacting with legislators and endorsing mental health legislation.

By making these changes, we can pave the way for a day when mental health is recognized, valued, and encouraged, and when people who suffer from anxiety feel free to ask for assistance without worrying about being judged or stigmatized. Although the road ahead is difficult, we can achieve significant progress in creating a society that is more inclusive and compassionate if we work together and are committed to the cause.